# A Poetic Inventory
of the Sandia Mountains

*poems by*

# Amaris Feland Ketcham

*Finishing Line Press*
Georgetown, Kentucky

# A Poetic Inventory
of the Sandia Mountains

Copyright © 2019 by Amaris Feland Ketcham
ISBN 978-1-64662-007-4 First Edition
All rights reserved under International and Pan-American Copyright Conventions. No part of this book may be reproduced in any manner whatsoever without written permission from the publisher, except in the case of brief quotations embodied in critical articles and reviews.

## ACKNOWLEDGMENTS

The following poems have been published by these literary magazines and anthologies:

"American Kestrel," *South85 Journal*
"Black Bear," *Qu Literary Magazine*
"Datil Yucca," *Thin Air*
"Lesser Stripetail Scorpion," "Ringtail Cat," *Bennington Review*
"Quakies: Populus Tremuloides," *Rooted: an Anthology of New Arboreal Writing*
"Rufous Hummingbird," *Rattle*
"Spear Globemallow," "Western Diamondback Rattlesnake," *The Kenyon Review*
"Tarantula Hawk Wasp," *Kudzu Review*

Publisher: Leah Maines
Editor: Christen Kincaid
Cover Art and Design: Amaris Feland Ketcham
Author Photo: Stephanie Stewart

Printed in the USA on acid-free paper.
Order online: www.finishinglinepress.com
also available on amazon.com

Author inquiries and mail orders:
Finishing Line Press
P. O. Box 1626
Georgetown, Kentucky 40324
U. S. A.

# Table of Contents

Roufus Hummingbird .......................................................................... 1

Black Bear ............................................................................................ 2

Chokecherry ........................................................................................ 4

Tarantula Hawk Wasp ........................................................................ 5

Western Diamondback Rattlesnake .................................................. 6

Cooper's Hawk .................................................................................... 7

Rocky Mountain Juniper .................................................................... 8

Ringtail Cat .......................................................................................... 9

American Kestrel .............................................................................. 10

Quaking Aspen .................................................................................. 11

Lesser Stripetail Scorpion ................................................................ 12

Desert Cottontail .............................................................................. 13

Ponderosa Pine ................................................................................. 14

Fendler's Hedgehog Cactus ............................................................. 15

Datil Yucca ........................................................................................ 16

Cane Cholla Cactus .......................................................................... 18

Greater Roadrunner ......................................................................... 19

Goat's Head ....................................................................................... 20

Claret Cup ......................................................................................... 21

Spear Globemallow .......................................................................... 23

## Rufous Hummingbird
*Selasphorus rufus*

Dear Albuquerque Garden Center,
Last month I purchased a hummingbird feeder
for $19.95. It was just like the original Lawrence J. Webster
designed for his wife in Boston in 1929. I filled the feeder
with one part refined white sugar and four parts water.
Well, the homemade nectar has fermented in the July heat
and all the little birds swerve in the sky. They're saying
the present doesn't exist. What is a current moment
when your heart beats 1200 times per minute?
As Janis said from the train, *Tomorrow never happens.
It's all the same fucking day, man.* Birds got their own
ball and chain. For the hummingbirds, it's an improv
of locating yourself. Please hurry. Don't walk.
Fly with 53 wingbeats per second, all in a figure 8,
a flapping Möbius strip. They've broken through infinity.
If your unshaven face flushes red with drink,
they'll join you on the patio. They buzz by your ears
with sayings about the space-time, typically called "now,"
and ask you to ask yourself, "when am I?" When
you perceive the present, it's already a recollection.
The rufous and I send you this thank you note
from the past; we will recommend the Webster feeder to all
our immediate friends who are happening over, over again.

## Black Bear
*Ursus americanus*

*once a woman went to the mountain alone*
1. NEVER say its name aloud, or you will wake the b    from hibernation.
2. Never feed    intentionally or accidentally.
    a. DO NOT leave prickly pear jams, fireweed honeys, or bushels of berries unattended at the picnic ground.
3. DO NOT walk into the woods alone carrying a bouquet of dainty coral bells, wild mountain iris, or even common daisies.
4. Look for a juniper branch at least ten feet off the ground to store fragrant items.

*to gather chokecherries*

5. Carry    mace with you at all times. The spray should project at least fifteen paces.
NEVER spray mace upwind.
6. DO NOT surprise    . DO NOT hide behind pine trees flirtatiously.
7. Stay on marked, well-traveled trails. Whistle while you walk or wear a small bell that jingles.
8. Learn to identify scat. It often smells peppery. Visible in the scat will be the seeds of prickly pear tunas and usually, small bells.

*she was abducted by a b—*
9. If you encounter a    , stay calm.
10. If you see a    in the distance, tell it a charming story about its kin eating from a picnic basket. Or do the Macarena so it will recognize you as human.

*they married*

11. If the b    charges at you, it is most likely bluffing. Stand your ground and it will pout that you are not reacting the way it wants.
12. ~~DO NOT run from the be~~  :
DO NOT run from the    .

*her sons were half-man, half-b—*

13. If the       attacks, be aggressive and fight back. Punch him in his Roman nose and kick him in the shins.

    a. If you brought a basket with berries, smoked salmon, honey drizzled across a baguette, and a juicy merlot blend, were you asking for it?

*one day, her brothers came for her*

14. If fighting back doesn't work, play dead by lying facedown, spread-eagle. Imagine yourself decomposing, falling into Mother Earth.

*revenge, bloodthirst, spear*

15. If you are mauled, rest assured it will be added to his record once if they locate him. All bears are given a second chance ("     will be    ") but after three strikes, many      are banished to Mount Taylor.

*the b—'s last words to her:*

16. Only one      has escaped exile. He walked 70 miles back to the Sandias. It is rumored that this      organizes raids on homes in the foothills. Its gang is said to lick barbecue grills clean, scavenge through compost piles, and wash their meals down with sugar water from hummingbird feeders.

*drape my hide so my head hangs toward the setting sun*
*and shadows lengthen behind me*

## Chokecherry
*Prunus virginiana*

Let me tell you the medicines
once used: drink sarsaparilla root
three times a day while wrapped in a saddle blanket,
sweating it out, to treat PMS, cramps,
and excessive menstrual bleeding. Copal resin
smoke creates incense that purifies, cures
fever and black widow bites. Infusions of horsetail
for kidney stones or to clean pots and pans,
decoctions of yerba del indio for snakebites
or scorpion stings, macerations and tinctures
of wildcrafted osha to quell swelling, kill fungus,
disinfect, release the bladder and the bowels,
and induce perspiration. Gather bark
and wood chips: strain a tea of kidneywood; take
a bath in palo del muerto; make a liniment of ocote
or candlewood. Chaparral, poinsettia,
willow groundsel, Mexican morning glory,
and wormwood came with blackbox warnings.
What the Spanish brought: manzanilla
for sleepytime tea, rosemary to keep
away the plague or disinfect the floors.
Curanderas and massage therapists-in-training
scour the foothills. They will make chokecherry wine.
In Las Huertas Canyon the bushes host a black fungus
that forms cankers on stems, and in large quantities
foliage can result in hydrogen cyanide poisoning.
But the wine isn't too sweet
and if taken at night, chokecherry treats those dreams
where you're in a bar on the Turquoise Trail,
the biker with hippie hair sings
you into the mineshaft
and you drop down, down, down.

### Tarantula Hawk Wasp
*Pepsis grossa*

Every wasp is a gazelle in its mother's eyes. Females sting
a tarantula and paralyze it. "She suffered an injury
to her back." The tarantula hawk wasp is the second
most painful insect sting in the world,
after the South American bullet ant. Justin O. Schmidt,
entomologist at the University of Arizona and creator
of the Schmidt Sting Pain Index, described it as "Blinding,
fierce, shockingly electric. A running hair drier
has been dropped into your bubble bath."
But he said the ant's sting was "Pure,
intense, brilliant pain. Like fire-walking
over flaming charcoal with a 3-inch rusty nail
grinding into your heel." He tried to stay drunk
for twelve hours to quell the pain, but his agony remained
strong. Then they drag it underground
through a pothole in Route 66. The mother lays an egg
in the tarantula and this larva nurses
on the paralyzed spider. From in-"not" +
jus (gen. juris) "right, law." Her children will be bright
blue with rusty orange wings. Colloq. a slap in the face,
two stabs in the back don't make a right. I wonder,
did it feed on your mother's memories or was she,
like us, born without history?

## Western Diamondback Rattlesnake
*Crotalus atrox*

Three things it is best to avoid: a flash flood, a strange dog,
and a Youtube comment thread.

Not everyone would tell it the same way.

My mother would advise you stay away
from a Baptist, a mean snake, and a cop—
though those are often the same thing.

Rattlesnakes have their own list: a diving hawk,
the heel of a hiking boot, a drunk frat boy.

At a different time, I may have told you:
Beware the corner of Tramway and San Bernardino.
There's a different ecosystem at that intersection.

That's the arroyo's entrance to a network of drainage tunnels.
College students call it the Devil's Den. Graffiti shows
Jesus, crucified and exclaiming "Don't tread on me!"

Teens rebel, drink Coors down there, use condoms, leave needles
everywhere. It's darkly festive. One rush of water and you're drowned
there: remember, an inch of rain

swings off the mountain, dives downtown to flood
knee deep. Beware a shirtless man crying near the light.
He's more afraid of you than you are of him

and that makes him dangerous. He's an ambush
predator. Beware your curiosity. He's rattled.
He blends in with cryptic markings: Zia symbols

and skull tattoos. Soon enough he'll leave
sunning on the sidewalk for a nap in the desert grassland.
He would tell you three things best to avoid:

a friend who's a rat, an ex who burns like wildfire,
and an intersection where wilderness swells in a city street.

**Cooper's Hawk**
    *Accipiter cooperii*

Returning to the spiritual center
of neck tattoos, pit bulls, and Bud
clamato, my friend walks past his old house
everyday at the intersection a new resident

lives in the front yard, second cottonwood
in the dead upper branches
like a (w) omen of danger
a few stiff wingbeats to glide

after an easy meal picked
off at the bird feeder
not a sunflower or thistle seed
she prefers

drowning doves in the birdbath.
A quarter of Cooper's hawks have healed
fractures on their wishbones. A promise breaks
in her red eye, steely stare, she swoops

bops him on his head. To be fair
his hair, color of a coyote; hers,
a dark executioner's hood. With slate gray
feathers and certain stealth

she cares for downy white hatchlings.
The city says they'd put up caution tape
but being private property they can't rope off
someone else's memory of home untethering.

### Rocky Mountain Juniper
*Juniperus scopulorum*

Robin, Autumn, Love—wait, throw it out.
How different would that line read
if the birds changed? Mourning Dove,

Autumn, Love. A different bird
has such personality. The season? Rosy
Finch, Winter, Brrrrr or something

more descriptive? Tiny Bones
in a Fur Ball at my Doorstep, Almost Halloween,
Smell of Green Chiles Roasting

little more than a memory.
That juniper out front? Smells
like gin, makes your eyes swell

and your throat scratchy, sentry
over centuries of drought. Some live
3,000 years, watch as your roommate moves

to the West Side, Southwestern suburbia
all strip malls bulldozed over
Indian graveyards. Takes a long time

to get there and then there's nothing
to do on a Friday night. Some observe
the mountains disappear, flurry

of elm seeds, silhouettes of birds, gust of desert
sand. Even cities on the edge mature autumnally
adobe begins as dust and ends

as another sandstone strata
in a complicated history
clawed and veined by roots.

## Ringtail Cat
### *Bassariscus astutus*

In the sunsquint, the ringtail re-dreams
his childhood: ricocheting
between sandstone ledges and cartwheeling
through Bear Canyon. How he learned
to trust his own two feet
when rotating them 180 degrees
and climbing down a dead juniper
headfirst. Sundown to sunup he lived
for a while as a miner's pet, mousing
the cabin all night and sleeping
in a small, dark box by the woodstove.

I saw a replica once: 100% real
composite ringtail. White mask, goofy
pink ears, muzzle that resembles a fox
and ringed tail as long as its body.
The twilit eyes were marbles, I guess,
but I searched them anyway
for a hint of his inner life.

All his ghost stories and nightmares
are sunlit, when the world blinds:
the sounds (that laughter, the crunch
of juniper cones underfoot) near, but
he cannot see the source. Milky whiteness
strips the world of playful shadows, his claws
protract, he might bolt
upright and bark, sleep shinny
away from this horrid radiance.

In the Natural History Museum
he posed on a severed branch, mid
day terror, eyes wide as if scanning the room
for an eternal exit through the burning light.

## American Kestrel
*Falco sparverius*

Millions of locusts swarmed
a mile deep—overhead they show bright green
on the meteorologist's radar, with yellow
highlights and neon blue fringes, a tropical storm
where Jim Morrison's face emerges then breaks
up over downtown because fewer trees trap less heat.
The American kestrel who sits on my telephone
wire grows fat and sleepy with this weatherman's plague.
The petite falcon just last month had a worried look,
a stain of running mascara down her eyes; she kleed,
whined, and chittered in the midday heat.
He stayed in the semiopen desert hills,
here and there abandoned lots; his heart
didn't seem into it anymore. Maybe
because I was calling him a sparrow hawk
or a grasshopper hawk, but the false eyes
on his back increased his stillness. Not a pocket mouse
nor a whiptail lizard moved.
Their nestlings began talking after sixteen
days, saying Killy killy killy, as they fed
on the mile of locusts.

## Quaking Aspen
### *Populus tremuloides*

The quaking aspen are a medium
not the message. Don't mistake an aspen's tremble
for the wind or a showy yellow leaf for autumn.
Wind shivers through them

just as a wave is not the water, but force
shoving the lake to lap the shore.
On the flesh of the medium shepherds have written
clues for the flock, directions, and preferences

for willing women. These notes won't last longer than papyrus,
sandstone, or your url. But they will outlive bathroom graffiti
written in Sharpie along the stall walls at the High Noon Saloon.
The aspen are also a message, not the medium. Like a scab of the mountains'

recent wound, they pioneer a new colony
after each forest fire. Aspen share a single root
system, a net of suckers a thousand years old. Each colony its own
clone; each tree identical to the next; each a trunk of the same organism.

And if the message is dieback, shared vulnerability
etched in their rhizome? Every aspen you've seen could disappear
at the same instant. So through the smooth white bark scarred
black; let the leaves tremble in your wake.

## Lesser Stripetail Scorpion
*Vaejovis coahuilae*

Some important notes about scorpion husbandry:
all scorpions look alike, misidentified

by pet store clerks and other teenage entomologists
analyzing florescence under black light. Consult a copy
of *Catalogue of the Scorpions of the World 1758-1998*

collected at your local Goodwill
shoved between Al Hurricane tapes and Carebear VHS.

Mothers, cannibalistic for 430 million years. It's hard

to find prey small enough
for early instars to eat, wingless fruit flies

must be mail-ordered purchased, bred
as food, or pinhead crickets can be served
freshly killed and ground, or you can just allow

the young to cannibalize one another
until you have an instar one inch and a half long
with a solid flick and run defense.

On a scale of 1-5 skulls and crossbones

he should have two: mild with edema, pain
lasting only thirty minutes in most adults

envenomations still lethal
to grandparents and little boys

who stick their pudgy fingers
deep where they don't belong.

### Desert Cottontail
*Sylvilagus audobonii*

Again upon a time, we look at defenses.
The washed-yellow desert cottontail dashes
across the trail, his alert white tail a signal
of danger for buffy tan brethren. Watch

the hawk, steer clear of the snake, sidestep
this coyote. Darwinists say the greatest defense

is an offense: rusty bunnies shield themselves
through their distinctive reproduction rate, but could it be
that they are self-replicating in spacetime? When pursued

the bunny will double back. It retraces time.
Sure they climb or swim when given

chase, but a burrow is a tunnel with two ends, each
at separate points in spacetime: synchronized clocks
show you exited at a point in time prior to your arrival,
perhaps a few feet into ten minutes ago,

a different desert universe, an outlet in time
where you might emerge as furless, blind, and unable
to hop as the day you were born.
Even the feces loops back again, re-ingested

for whatever nutrients didn't stick to the ribs
the first time around. Just look in the tall grass
and forbs: here's the glint of an ever-growing incisor,

an error in duplication, before this pale gray meals-on-wheels
starts each chase anew, anew, anew.

**Ponderosa Pine**
*Pinus ponderosa*

One girl stood among a spill of bones
in the forest she couldn't see for the pines. A long green needle
pricked one's heart. One peeled
back scaly red bark

to smell its secret inner vanilla.
Oh no, it's that dream where you've forgotten to put on pants
and look, your legs are covered in sap.
One thought she saw a golden eagle soaring

to a prickly pear but it was only a vulture
spiraling. Did the rapture take a rain check last week
or was she left behind and just didn't notice
the vanishing of the good

given her preference for complicated people? All
she has is this stack of photos
not one candid or printed. These memories
formed like rust, only in neglect

flakes itched off in disregard.
One confused her palm print for a map, left walking
following her life line through the sagebrush
only to enter another cemetery

of mothers, aunts, grandmothers
who were told they had no wilderness
in them and disappeared
in a forest of skinny shadows.

One went looking for redemption
but all she got was another forest fire. She climbed

the ponderosa pine
hugging it like a black bear

the bark scraped and bloodied her thighs
but ah, how fresh was the morning air.

### Fendler's Hedgehog Cactus
*Echinocereus fendleri*

Imagine that once a year
when the weather started to get nice
a giant magenta flower grew
out of your crown
doubling your height
tickled by bees
petals ruffled by wind
gold dust pollen dancing in the air
oblivious to history
licking its chapped lips.

## Datil Yucca
### *Yucca baccata*               *—for Zaira*

When La Virgen appeared
in a bent yucca stalk
in the city sprawl

nearly four hundred years after coming
to Tepeyac on a woven yucca cloth
framed by rigid spine-tipped leaves

in dry rocky meadows
when La Lupe used to speak Nauhautl,
before she adapted

to staying silent
and showing up on tortillas
(she has her reasons

for sidestepping potatoes and rye loaves)
La Virgen emerged as a slender
silhouette in a bent yucca stalk.

She likes a ruckus
when she comes back
crowds coveting temperance, Ave Marias

pumped from low-rider stereos
down the main drag. Only
the devout light votive candles

to cure their shock
when seeing yucca casting her shadow
against the crosswalk not some metaphor

about her grace being the breeze
bowing the hollyhock. You can do anything
with yucca. Its roots make soap

and shampoo or a laxative
too strong to be consumed.
In midsummer, chew

drooping waxy flowers raw (pollinated
by small nocturnal moths
who deposit eggs in blooms

where larva ingest the seeds)
to relieve arthritis. From the fiber
you can make sandals, buckets,

or weave a new world goddess
whose name glows on your tongue
like an ancient language

snatched by a hawk and dropped
in an inaccessible rocky outcrop forever
creeping back in another yucca stalk.

## Cane Cholla Cactus
*Cylindropuntia imbricata*

There are three types of déjà vu.
1. The classic, "already seen," déjà vu everyone knows:
*You have been here before*

on this trail. Note the cairn with three handsome stones,
the cholla garden, the praying mantis with short wings.
Even here you'll find silk flowers
deadheaded from plastic stems
at the cemetery. Have you seen this lily
skim across the road while running
in a dream?

2. Jamais vu: *a common situation goes unrecognized.*
How many times do you say a word before it loses
meaning? Say damselfly damselfly damselfly
or dragonfly or their larvae, nymph nymph nymph,
ten times fast and get back to me.

For example, a prince fought through the field of cholla
cholla cholla brambles to save the drugged beauty.
She: poisoned by yellow cactus fruit in *sauce Robert*.
Or did she prick her finger? He: a thousand barbs
broke his dreadfully white skin, the flowers, too,
were bright magenta. Did he hide his face
in the hall of mirrors before falling to his knees? They kiss
and she wakes, but the princess does not fit back in its box.

3. Presque vu: *the brink of an epiphany.*
Remember the name of whatshisface,
your pure teenage love? Relish the sensation
as his memory lingers on the tip of your tongue
before your brain and vocal chords catch up.

In all the old photos you were always in the background
climbing out of a window. She emerged as you were
leaving. Sometimes all you have to show for a decade is a promise
of absence and the unbreakable
bundle of cholla cholla cholla skeletons.

## Greater Roadrunner
### *Geococcyx californianus*

Mixed blessings feed on blessings
in cartoon physics, the jurisdiction of details

until he realizes it
he lives to try again
coyote doesn't fall. Who was watching?

Kids in a Chevy truck. TNT bought
in Moriarty. Rocket from the air
force base. Bear trap in the foothills.
Which Acme device will be his destruction?
Most often it's velocity not the laws of gravity.

Through a door painted on rock he ducked
lifting his crest how Groucho raises his eyebrows.
Which way did he go?

Evil spirits can't tell     forward or backward
they look the same      His tracks
scratch X's in the sand.
He's blessed, no? We see the Other

in roadrunner; in coyote

we see ourselves. Beyond his niche
curiosity and hunger stretch coyote
into a failure. The song dog?

Gift limpened in his sharp beak
lizard smacked against pavement for one
lady roadrunner. Who led him here?

It must have been noon. Yellow sky.
City of burnt orange cliffs. Roadrunner
lured. Chevy rocketing downroad. Another
tight escape. Children clapping wildly.

**Goat's Head**
*Tribulus terrestris*

I cuss like a sailor threading
a bobbin, searching for a destination

with Apple maps, or stepping
on a goat head. Damn little burrs,

size of a pill, two devilish
horns long enough to puncture

bicycle tires and leave a wound
as deep and round as a thumbtack.

In Latin, the weed's name means "spiky
weapon." Heed it's tiny lemon-yellow

flowers. Stems branch radially, flat
along the ground, patchy covering

across sidewalks, laying in wait
to surprise the sole. Invasive

in the poor soil of waste sites, disturbed lots
like the lawn of my home.

## Claret Cup Cactus
*Echinocereus triglochidiatus*

Not my arms[1] but the brown that hugs you
close[2], crisscrosses your body and flirts
with your imagination: what does the next switchback
promise? Love and a stomp of cactus[3] with bright red buds.
Spring wind[4] to bedevil your hair and enough sun
to make you sweat. Hold summer in your breast
and hope to come by its cupped blossoms honestly.[5] Lie
sandstone[6] still for we are not limited by light

---

[1] New Mexico holds a unique tricultural position in the history of the United States.—Myra Ellen Jenkins & Albert H. Schroeder, *A Brief History of New Mexico* (1974)

[2] Although a modern reader might surmise that "New Mexico" is derived directly from the place name "Mexico," as we now identify that modern country, it has instead a somewhat more complicated history.—Mary Montano, *Tradiciones Nuevomexicanas: Hispano Arts and Culture of New Mexico* (2001)

[3] Seeing New Mexico as the Savage Reservation and, along with the rest of the arid West, as a national sacrifice zone, helps us to understand environmental racism.—V.B. Price, *The Orphaned Land: New Mexico's Environment Since the Manhattan Project* (2011)

[4] Trinity stands for the Christian culture of the Spanish and later the Anglo Americans as well as for the Trinity site in White Sands, where the world's first atomic bomb was detonated on July 16, 1945.—ed. Marta Weigle and Peter White, *The Lore of New Mexico* (2003)

[5] Living in extraordinary times, and doing extraordinary things, these people have kept alive the possibilities that we have all but forgotten ever existed—the possibility for hope coming through simple faith, for change coming about through rituals, and for miracles.—Eliseo "Cheo" Torres, *Curandero: A Life in Mexican Folk Healing* (2005)

[6] One day, you can be sweltering in the desert backcountry of Carlsbad Caverns National Park, the next you can be shivering at an alpine lake as snow flurries shroud the peaks above.—Laurence Parent, *Hiking New Mexico: A Guide to 95 of the State's Greatest Hiking Adventures* (2011)

but a collection of dust and woolly barbs
of memory. Beyond the next rocky outcrop[7] perhaps
the flowers stay open all night, pink stamens solicit birds
among the bristles, perhaps men are softer
there: mighty winds[8] rearrange their troubles.
Sorries erode and vanish by year's end. A bleary love[9]
circles. Best to fall back and fade[10] into the foothill's soft
brown curves. Take this long needle from the claret cup
and try to scratch the patina off your last epiphany[11].

---

[7] When Captain E. F. Dutton and his party rode into this glorious country in the 1880s to survey it for the for the U.S. Geological Survey, he found the terms of his own language—"hill," "valley," "mountain"—too puny to describe what he saw.—Sherry Robinson, *El Malpais, Mt. Taylor, and the Zuni Mountains: A Hiking Guide and History* (1994)

[8] The most important natural area in New Mexico exists wherever one goes in the state. It is the sky overhead.—ed. Marta Weigle, *Telling New Mexico: A New History* (2009)

[9] Early Spanish explorers called them Sandia, "watermelon," a descriptive name for the rugged mountains that blush deep rose pink at sunset and form an ever-changing backdrop for the city of Albuquerque.—ed. Stephen G. Maurer, *Visitors Guide Sandia Mountains: Cibola National Forest Sandia Ranger District* (1994)

[10] Fifty years ago, more or less, I was first made aware that Sandia Mountain was something magical-mystical, and not merely for the solid physical reasons a lot of us like to live in Albuquerque.—eds. Robert Julyan and Mary Stuever, *Field Guide to the Sandia Mountains* (2005)

[11] Sometimes, even today, I'm surprised that I live in a place called Albuquerque—and that I call it home.—V.B. Price, *Albuquerque: A City at the End of the World* (2003)

## Spear Globemallow
### *Sphaeralcea hastulata*

In the mirror broken cottonwoods
are closer than they appear, then gone.
"Look, it's the New Mexico wildflower!"
He points to a Wal-Mart bag bloomed from sagebrush.
A beer can birthed from yucca. If the earth laughs
in flowers, it weeps in litter. Following his finger, I see
little orange flowers. They grow from a downy clump
of muted green; their orange petals cup a column
of stamens. They bloom from last frost to first, niching
the whole city's expanse from river to mountain.
As wild as a wildflower gets. I've heard
the globemallow is good for sore throats, rashes, and memories
where you are always looking the other way.

**Amaris Feland Ketcham** is an Honorary Kentucky Colonel who now resides in Albuquerque, NM. She is usually involved in some combination of open space, white space, CMYK and RGB, flash nonfiction, long trails, f-stops, line breaks, and several Adobe programs running simultaneously. Her work has appeared in *Creative Nonfiction,* the *Kenyon Review,* the *Los Angeles Review, Prairie Schooner, Rattle,* and the *Utne Reader*, and many more print and online journals. She has also painted murals in Albuquerque, performed as a cast member on a radio drama for the Badlands National Park, and developed the creative place-making project, Poetic Routes (www.poeticroutes.com). Atlas in hand, she is currently researching and writing the third edition of "Best Tent Camping: New Mexico," forthcoming from AdventureKEEN. You can find out more at her website, www.amarisketcham.com.

www.ingramcontent.com/pod-product-compliance
Lightning Source LLC
LaVergne TN
LVHW041521070426
835507LV00012B/1727